NORTHUMBRIAN CASTLES

WANSBECK AND COQUET

SERIES 3

by **FRANK GRAHAM**

© 1974

SBN 902833 67 7

Northern History Booklets No. 31

Published by Frank Graham, 6 Queen's Terrace, Newcastle upon Tyne, NE2 2PL
Printed by Howe Brothers (Gateshead) Ltd.

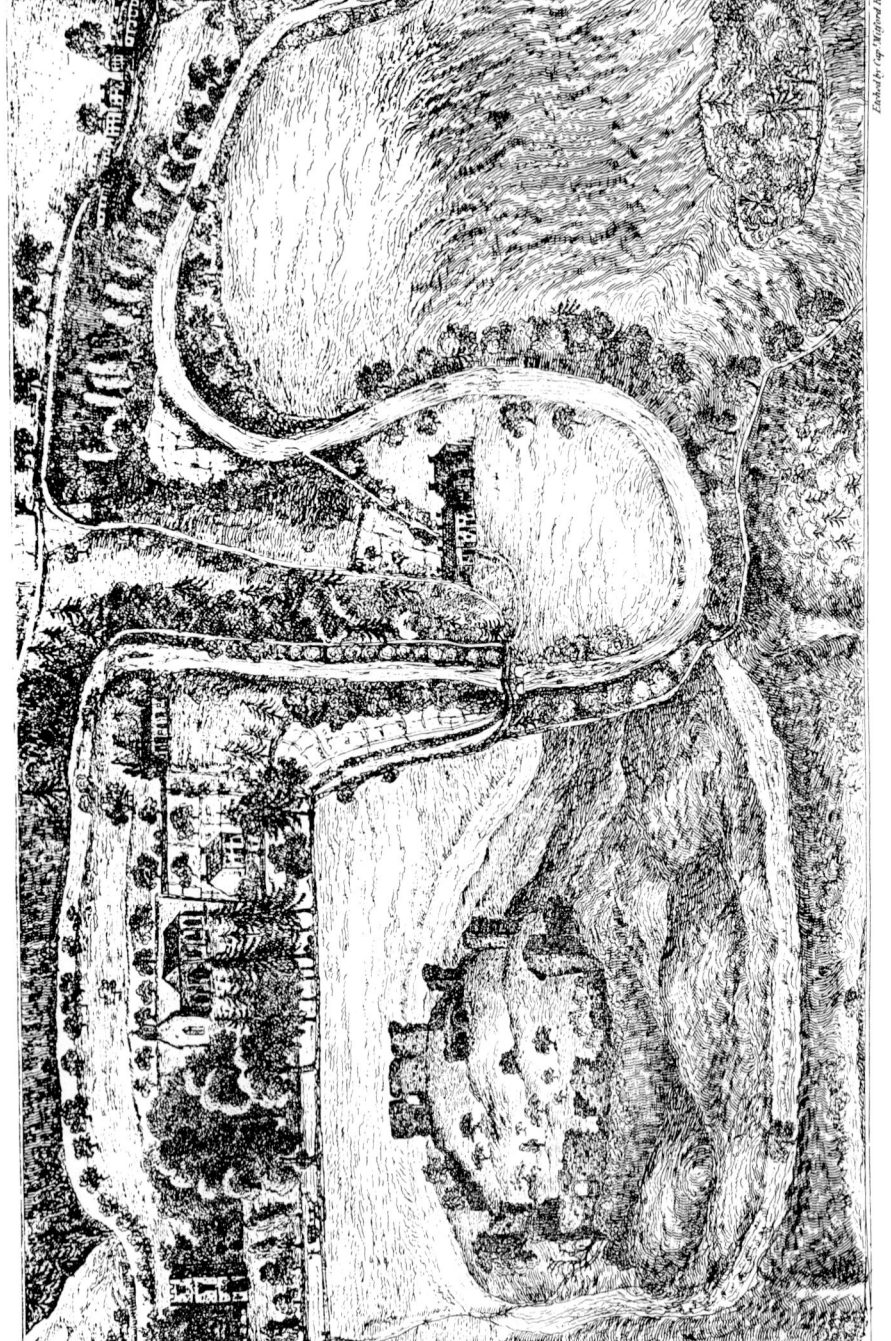

Bird's Eye-view of Mitford, 1832

Etched by Capt Mitford R.N.

ALNHAM TOWER (Upper Coquetdale)

The tower belonged to the Earl of Northumberland and is first mentioned in 1405. In 1532 the earl reported that:—

> Scots — to the number of 300 personages and above hathe brunte a toune of mine called Alenam with all the corne, hay and householde stuff in the said toune and also a woman'.

The Border Survey of 1541 reported both the towers as being in disrepair. In Stockdale's Survey of the Earls lands in 1586 we read the following interesting remarks:—

> Alnham. The Lord hath there a faire stronge stone Tower of Ancient tyme builded and strongly vaulted over and the Gates and Dores be all of great strong Iron Barres and a good demayne adjoining thereto, the House is now ruinous and in some decay by reason the Farmer useth to carry his sheep up the Stares and to lay them in the Chambers which rotteth the Vaultes and will in shorte time be the utter decay of the same house if other reformacion be not had.

Dixon tells us that the foundations of this extensive fortress were still visible 80 years ago on a green hill opposite the church showing traces of a square tower, remains of other buildings and the wall of the barmekyn.

ALNHAM VICAR'S PELE

The Vicar's pele lies to the west of the church. It is mentioned in 1541 as a "lytle toure" the mansion of the vicarage. It was ruinous in 1663 and likewise in 1758 when the vicar resided at Ilderton. The tower was of fourteenth century workmanship with tunnel-vaulted ground floor, walls nine feet thick and unusually ornate window openings. In 1821 John Hodgson made a sketch of it which we reproduce. Shortly afterwards the tower was restored, parapets were added and all the windows re-done. A modern wing was built, it is now a youth hostel.

ALWINTON: BASTLE HOUSE OF VICAR

The vicar of Alwinton (Upper Coquetdale) like many other border parsons lived in a fortified house in medieval times. In 1541 we read; "At Allaynton ys a lytle bastell house of stone the mansion of the vicaredge scaresly in good repac'ons.." Early in the 17th century John Hearon, a descendant of a well-known Northumbrian family took possession of the vicar's bastle house and let is as an alehouse so that the vicar had to build himself a small cottage to live in. The bastle fell into decay and to-day the site is no longer known.

BARROW TOWER

On the other side of the Coquet, half a mile from Alwinton is Barrow Farm, marked on the ordnance survey map as a pele tower. But nothing remains of the old fortress. In 1522 a garrison of 20 men was stationed here but in 1541 we read: "At Barrowe a lytle above Harbottel upon the southe syde of the said ryver of Cokett standeth the old walles of a lytle fortresse of the Inherytance of one Gerrard Barrowe which in tyme past was brounte and rased by the Scottes in a warre tyme. And so remaineth still waste because the oweners thereof have bene but poor men and not able nor of power sythens to reparell the same."

BEBSIDE HALL

The old hall at Bebside of which only a fragment remains was a hundred feet in length. It incorporated a tower of an earlier date measuring 20 by 30 feet. Most of the old hall was demolished about the year 1853 and the material used for building farm cottages.

BEDLINGTON OLD HALL

This sixteenth century tower house had hood moulded mullioned windows. It was demolished in 1959.

BELSAY CASTLE

There is no record of the date of the building of Belsay Castle but it was probably early in the fifteenth century. The manor of Belsay came into the hands of the Middleton family in 1240 and except for a brief period in the possession of Sir John de Strivelyn, (the man who probably started the building of the castle) has remained in their hands to the present day.

The tower is rectangular in plan and 56 feet x 47 feet in size, with walls nine feet thick at the base, being one of the largest in the county. At each corner is a turret which do not oversail the corners but project beyond the side walls in five courses. Between the corners are machicolated battlements and similar but lower battlements also crown the turrets. One of the bartizans in the south west corner is square and contains the newel staircase. It is higher than the other corner towers, a

Doorway opening onto stair from Great Hall

R.W.THOMPSON

Vaulted roof of staircase

Belsay Castle from the North

similar arrangement being found at Cockle Park. Buck's View of 1728 shows a ruined outlying corner tower which may have been the remains of a fortified barmkin. The main tower has three floors one above the other. The lowest has a pointed tunnel vault and was used as a kitchen. Above this is the Hall with two large two-light windows, a fireplace and remains of mural decoration. Painting on the wall was common in medieval castles but little has survived. The third storey is the upper hall also with a fireplace. In the north-western corner are four small rooms and six of still smaller size in the south western corner which also contains the staircase.

A more comfortable house was added to the west side, covering the entrance, at an early date. The renaissance doorway with coupled

Truscan columns was built in 1614 when alterations were made to this mansion. An inscription above stated: "Thomas Middleton and Dorothy his wife builded this house 1614".

The nearby Belsay Hall was built 1810-17 by Sir Charles Monck with plans by John Dobson. Since the family have now left this Hall to live in a modernised farmhouse on the estate, Belsay is in the position of having a family dwelling in four stages of development over 600 years.

Large room in the basement of Belsay Castle

BIDDLESTONE TOWER

Two miles from the village of Netherton stands the lonely tower of Biddlestone which is built on the top of a slope and commands a fine prospect of the vale of the Coquet and the hills beyond. Here once stood Biddlestone Hall, said to be the Osbaldistone Hall of Rob Roy. But the Hall with its flourishing groves of oak and pine have gone. "For more than six hundred years the Selbys have been at Biddlestone. The first of the name on record is Sir Walter de Selby, to whom Edward I granted the lands of Biddlestone forfeited by William Vissard. The

7

next Sir Walter, together with Sir John and Sir Gilbert Middleton, disclaimed the authority of Edward II and took all the castles in the county with three exceptions. One affair in which he was concerned was peculiarly audacious. As the Bishop of Durham was escorting two legates from the Pope through his diocese, the three comrades in arms fell on the stately cavalcade at Rushyford, between Woodham and Ferryhill, rifled the Romish cardinals and bore off the Bishop to Mitford Castle. In 1346 Sir Walter was governor of Liddel Castle, and with the small force under him, resisted for six days the attacks of Robert Bruce and his army of 40,000 Scots. For this gallant defence he and his garrison were cruelly put to the sword". Tomlinson.

The tower is mentioned in 1415 and 1541. The lower walls still exist on which the family chapel of the Selbys was built at the beginning of the 19th century. While some alterations were being made in 1879 a secret passage was discovered in the thickness of the wall. The walls were 6 feet thick and the tower measures 42 by 32 feet. A built-up doorway at the ground level in the east wall gave access to the stone-vaulted basement.

A modern Border ballad written by Hogg, the Ettrick Shepherd, mentions Biddlestone Tower. It described a raid of the Kerrs of Cessford into Coquetdale in 1549:—

> Their armour was light, but their brands were bright,
> And their bonnets were steel across the crown,
> And whenever they spied an Englishman,
> They gallop'd at him and put him down.

Biddlestone Tower

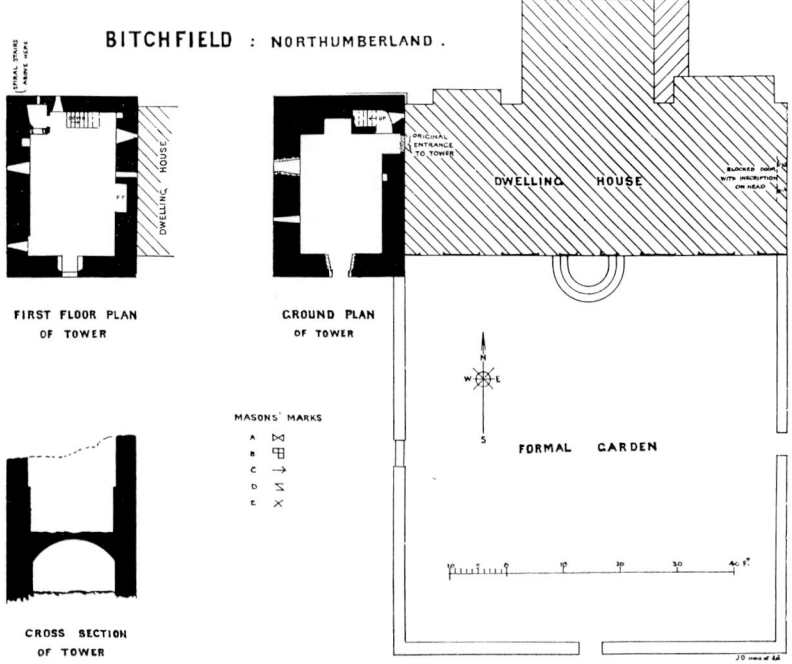

BITCHFIELD : NORTHUMBERLAND .

FIRST FLOOR PLAN
OF TOWER

GROUND PLAN
OF TOWER

DWELLING HOUSE

MASONS' MARKS

CROSS SECTION
OF TOWER

FORMAL GARDEN

From Archaeologia Aeliana

BITCHFIELD TOWER (Old English—Beechfield)

It is situated one mile wouth of Belsay Tower. There is no documen-
tary evidence of its history but clearly it was built in the 15th century.
A dwelling house was later added on the east side probably by Robert
Fenwick whose initials with the date 1622 can still be seen above the
door inside the kitchen. The door and windows of the front of the
house are very attractive with a walled garden in front entered by
ornamental gate-piers. The pele tower measures 31 feet by 23 feet. It
is tunnel-vaulted as usual and there are traces of a barmkin wall and a
moat on three sides. It has been completely restored and is now occupied.
Our drawing shows the tower before restoration.

BOLAM TOWER

On the top of Bolam hill is an oval enclosure defended by a ditch
and rampart. Whether it was an ancient British camp or contained
the residence of the early lords of Bolam barony we do not know.

Bitchfield Tower.

There is no visible evidence that it was ever a castle of the motte and bailey type. However a later medieval stone tower was built within the enclosure measuring 40 by 30 feet. The remnants of this tower and other buildings on the site were used as a quarry to build Bolam Hall.

The barony was held in 1168 by Gilbert of Bolam, later by the Caux family, and from 1248 until the early 15th century by Sir Thomas Bekering and his successors. In 1305 Bolam was granted a market and fair. There were once two hundred houses here round the village green but now only three mansions and a church (with Anglo-Saxon tower) survive.

BUTTER KNOWES BASTLE

In Rothbury Forest there used to be a number of strong houses which are described by Mackenzie, in his *View of Northumberland* published in 1825, as follows:—

"The whole forest is dotted over with solitary farmsteads, from a quarter of a mile to a mile distant from one another. These houses, or rather strongholds, are very old, and are usually called Peels. Here however, they are named *Bastle buildings*. The walls are in general about five feet thick, and the stones secured by strong cement, though sometimes mud has been used. The doors which are low and narrow, are usually placed at the east end of the building, the jambs of stone, with holes to receive a strong wooden bar, by which means the door was barred and the cattle secured on the ground floor: the light was admitted through loop-holes. The second floor is supported either by a stone arch, or thick oak joists; and was entered on the south side by stone steps, the door being fastened as below. Near the fire-place, and directly above the vault door, was a projection from the wall, contrived for the purpose of pouring down boiling water on the mass-troppers, who were assaulting the building below".

Butter Knowes and all the other batles have disappeared. Even the site is uncertain.

CADGER'S FORT, ROTHLEY

It was built in 1745 as a defence against the Stuart menace from Scotland. It is a mere parapeted breastwork of unhewn stone, over-looking Rothley Lake.

Cambo Pele

CAMBO TOWER

The picturesque village of Cambo stands in a commanding position beside the Rothbury to Hexham road. Cambo tower is now a Post Office and shop. The building is of three stories built of rubble and squared quoins. It measures 24 x 35 feet with walls $4\frac{1}{2}$ feet thick. It was remodelled in 1818 as the date on the lintel of the principal window informs us. However, even before that it was a shop. The Cambo Women's Institute Book, *In the Troublesome Times*, quotes George Handyside as follows:—

> "My father and grandfather had this shop before me, and before them it was kept by a warlock, and people daursn't owe him anything. There was a woman lived where our kitchen is now, and she kept a cow, and when she churned she used to lock the door for fear the warlock cast an evil eye on the milk and turned it sour. His shop was upstairs. That's his window that's walled up".

CAPHEATON CASTLE

A little to the south of the present hall there formerly stood a Border stronghold which Leland (1538) calls Hutton "a faire Castle in the midste of Northumberland, as in the Bredthe of it. It is IIII or V miles northe from Fenwicke Pile, and this is the oldist Howse of the Swynburnes".

Collins says it was "moated about and had a drawbridge, and was a place of resort in the moss-trooping times, when the gentlemen of the country met together to oppose those felonious aggressors upon the goods and chattels of the country, having a beacon on its top, to alarm the neighbourhood". It is first mentioned in 1415 but the manor and probably the castle already built was purchased by Allan de Swinburne from Sir Thomas de Fenwyke in 1274. The pele was demolished by the first baronet Sir John Swinburne in 1668 and the present mansion built nearby after the designs of Robert Trollop. (For a description of Capheaton Hall and Robert Trollop see "Tyneside Portraits" by Lyall Wilkes, 1971). The early life of Sir John Swinburne was rather unusual. We are told "that he was sent while a child to a monastery in France, where one of the Radcliffe family, accidently visiting the place, recognised in his face the features of the Swinburne family. On enquiring of the monks how he came there, the only answer they could give was that/he came from England, and that an annual sum was remitted for his board and education. On questioning the boy himself, it was however found that he had been told that his name was Swinburne, which with the account of his father's death, and his own mysterious disappearance in Northumberland, induced the superior of the house to permit him to return home, where, in an inquest specially empanelled for that purpose, he identified himself to be the son of John Swinburne and Ann Blount, by the description he gave of the marks upon a cat, and a punch-bowl, which were still in the house".

CARTINGTON CASTLE

Cartington Castle stands three miles NW of Rothbury controlling the Debdon pass over the Rothbury hills. It is first mentioned in 1415 and in the Survey of 1541 is described as a "good fortresse of two toures

CARTINGTON CASTLE.

and other stronge houses". In the reign of Elizabeth extensive alterations were carried out making it one of the largest and finest mansions
in Northumberland. It suffered badly during the Civil War but was
subsequently restored. In the 18th century it is referred to as a "hand-
some seat on the top of a hill well planted with trees" but before long
it became a ruin. In 1887 Lord Armstrong had the remains strengthened
and preserved. The architect C. C. Hodges has been criticised for his
work, perhaps unjustly, but some of the windows were probably never
in their present positions. It is now very difficult to disentangle the
various stages of the building.

The castle consists of a great square courtyard with a range of
buildings to the north, the east end of which is a lofty 14th century
tower. This tower measures 31 x 41 feet and has walls 6 feet thick. The
ground floor is a semi-circular barrel vault. The remainder of the north
wing is now at ground level divided into three large rooms.

On the south side of the courtyard are two towers the south east
one being the oldest and containing a guardrobe: the one on the south
west is barely visible.

CAUSEY PARK TOWER

Six miles north of Morpeth is the hamlet of Causey Park Bridge.
Half a mile to the west is Causey Park which is a late Georgian house.
It incorporates part of Causey Park Tower which was built by James
Ogle in 1586. Two of the spiral staircases survive. In the gardens is a
curious sun-dial surmounted by a globe, and having the arms of the
Lords Ogle on the one side, and on the other three sides the hemis-
pheres, phases of the moon and tables of the sun's rising and setting.
The dial is dated 1705.

CHOPPINGTON TOWER

The tower at Choppington, in Bedlingtonshire, was built by
Garven Ogle about 1503. It is first mentioned in the survey of 1541
but its site is now unknown.

CLENNEL HALL

A mile north of Alwinton is Clennel, an old pele tower modernised
into a delightful country residence. Clennel stands on the "Thieves
Rode" of the Middle Ages, called in the 18th century the Salters Road
of the smugglers, but its powerful walls have survived all vicissitudes.
The Border Survey of 1541 says:— "At Clennel ys a lytle toure of
thinherytaunce of one P'cyvall Clennel, gent, newly reparelled and
brattyshed by the same P'cyvall. And also he ys in makinge of a newe
barmeky nabout the same as his power will extende thereunto." Clennel
tower is not included in the 1415 list of Border fortresses, neither is
it mentioned in that of 1509. The Clennel family were long resident
in the area and in 1434 William Clennell was constable of Harbottle.

CLENNELL.

The tower is small being 22 by 30 feet with walls 6 feet thick. The ground floor is a stone arched basement with a fine loop at one end and an entrance door at the other with an ascending stair in the thickness of the wall. There was an upper floor and perhaps an attic. In 1568, as is shown by the date on the lintel of a doorway, a new wing was built running west. At the same time a storey was added to the old tower and its Tudor fireplace still remains. Further alterations were made in the 17th century but in 1895 the buildings were renovated and turned into the mansion we know today. The village of Clennel was cleared away to make room for the park and gardens. At Clennel Hall can be seen today "the most interesting bit of ancient work ever seen in Northumberland". It is a piece of Elizabethan plaster work representing a hunting scene. The panel of course has been brought here from elsewhere.

COCKLE PARK TOWER

A mile to the north of Hebron village, near Morpeth, is Cockle Park Tower, a fine 15th century pele converted into a farm house. The farm was called Bubbleymires. It was used as an experimental farm by the Northumberland County Council and Newcastle University but recently the building due to structural faults has been vacated.

The tower is oblong with bartizans corbelled out on the two north corners. Between the bartizans are machicolated battlements. The ground floor is vaulted with a spiral staircase. On the east front is a large stone tablet bearing the arms of Ogle quartering Bertram with two collared and chained antelopes, the supporters of the lords Ogle. The windows are Tudor and 18th century. Inside the tower are two curious old fireplaces.

15

COCKLE PARK TOWER, NORTHUMBERLAND.

ELLIBURN TOWER (Rothbury)

In the survey of 1541 we read that at Elyburne in the lordship of Rothbury was a strong pele house. The very name has now disappeared but it is thought the site was the Lee, a farmhouse on the Forest Burn, near which an old hollow way or ancient road runs.

FAIRNLEY PELE (Hartburn Parish)

Hodgson tells us that a pele with a vaulted basement and a room above stood in a farmyard at High Farneylaw on the north bank of the Hart burn.

FALLOWLEES BASTLE

Fallowlees lies on the slopes of Simonside five miles south of Rothbury. The survey of 1541 tells us that there was "no stone house buylded thereupon". But some time later a strong bastle house was built, whose foundations can still be traced.

FAWNS (SAWNS) PELE

"At the Sawnes is a lytle pele house or bastell" belonging to Sir John Fenwick (1541). This is the only reference to this pele at Fawnes, to the north of Wallington Hall.

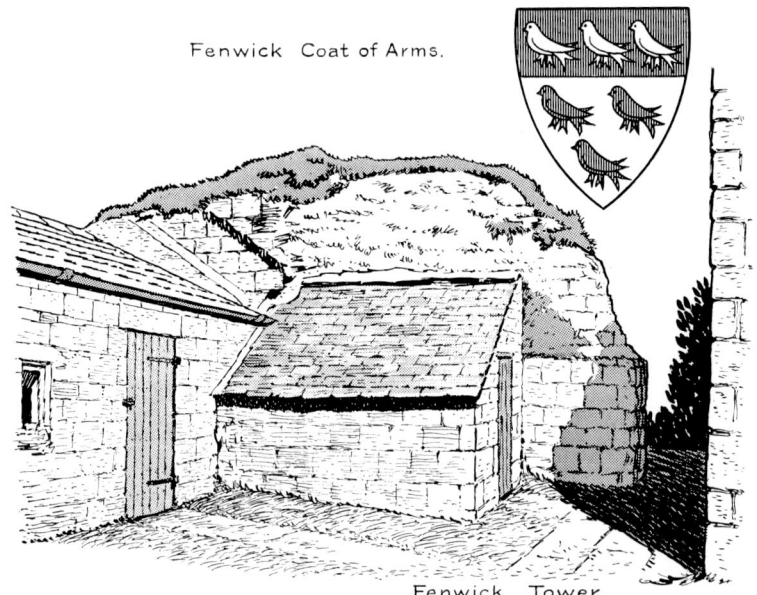

Fenwick Coat of Arms.

Fenwick Tower.

FENWICK TOWER

The name Fenwick means the "dwelling on the fen". There is no village but the remains of Fenwick Tower are built into a farmhouse which lies midway between Stamfordham and Matfen. Licence to crenellate was granted in 1378 to the ancient family of Fenwick, so celebrated in Border warfare. However shortly afterwards Wallington Hall became their "chiefest house". All that is now left is the vaulted basement.

Buried treasure was found here in 1775. We are told that "William Cooke, a labourer employed in taking down some part of Fenwick Tower found 226 broad pieces of gold coined for Edward III. Each piece was of the value of 20s., and they had probably been buried there by Sir John Fenwick who had two sons Alan and John prisoners in Scotland at the time of his death. The pieces were buried in sand, edgeways like a roll of dollars, under the pavement of a room above that which formed the stable for the cattle in the time of the invasion of the Scots. They were so fresh that they appeared as though just from the mint". The buried treasure is a great mystery. Where had Sir John obtained all this "new money" so suddenly. We know he

17

Fenwick Tower.
Sir John Hiding the Treasure.

died shortly after hiding the money, but why did he not tell any other member of his family? The story of this hoard of gold still remains to be discovered.

The last of the Fenwicks, Sir John, sold Fenwick tower to Sir Walter Blackett of Wallington in 1689. A few years later he was arrested for complicity in a plot to restore James II, and although every effort was made to save him he died by the headsman's axe on Tower Hill in 1695. He died childless.

GREAT TOSSON TOWER

The ruins of the border tower of the Ogles stands in the centre of the village of Great Tosson nearly opposite a house which was formerly the Royal George Inn. It appears to date from the 15th century but in 1541 was reported as "not in good rep'ac'ons". It was one of a line of towers extending from Harbottle to Warkworth. It was in size 42 by 36 feet with walls 9 feet thick. Although the large outer stones have been removed the rubble interior stands solid like concrete. A very good spring is nearby and this was probably inside the barmkin.

The Rev. John Hodgson wrote the following description of it about 1830:—

"Tosson Tower. Its vault still remains but the arch of it much broken, the outside ashlar and indeed almost the whole of the inside ones except the pining stone have been taken away. The masonry is good, the wall 8 feet thick, the inside as usual rudely enough filled with line, sand and rough stone all of which are strongly cemented together, the sand porphyry from the bed of the Coquet: has a doorway to the south east. Behind it on the south rises one of the Simonside hills which prevents the sun from shining upon it for nearly 3 months in the winter: to the north-east it has a fine view down upon Rothbury, Whitton Tower, Newtown, Thropton, Trewhit and the fertile and undulating land from Biddlestone to Rothley and from Snitter to the Cheviots. Thus Tosson stands proudly and darkly over the valley, has some trees about it: the stone of which the vill and tower are built excellent white sandstone".

GREENLEIGHTON BASTLE

Greenleighton is five miles due north of Wallington Hall. In the survey of 1541 it is described as a "lytle stone house" with its barmkin in decay. Nothing can be seen today.

HARBOTTLE CASTLE

Harbottle is one of the largest of Northumbrian castles and had a position of great importance in the defence of the border. This magnificent fortress, once the capital of the Lordship of Redesdale is now a complete ruin. There may have been a prehistoric camp on the site. However in 1157 Henry II instructed Odinel de Umfraville to build a castle here but probably before the work was finished in 1173 it was taken by the Scots, but in the next century rebuilt. In 1296 "Robert de Ros and the Earls of Athol and Menteith, with a horde of 40,000, besieged the castle for two days in rain, killing the deer in the park". One of the most interesting events occurred in 1515 when Lord Dacre was warden of the Middle Marches and resident there. Margaret of Scotland gave birth to a daughter here who was the grandmother of James I of England. Margaret seems to have been more interested in her clothes than her daughter. Lord Dacre described his situation as "uneaseful and costly, by occasion of the far carriage of everything, and so we were minded to move her Grace to Morpeth as soon as conveniently she may. Nevertheless, she has a wonderful love of apparel. She has caused the gown of cloth of gold and the gown of cloth of tynsen, sent by Henry, to be made against this time, and likes the fashion so well, that she will send for them, and have them held

Harbottle Castle in 1903

The Keep, Harbottle Castle 1903

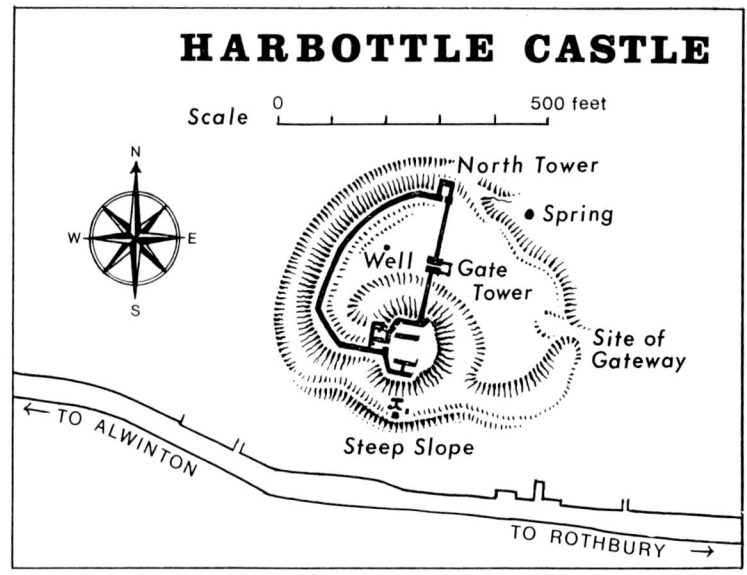

HARBOTTLE CASTLE

Scale 0 _____ 500 feet

N

W E

S

North Tower

Spring

Well Gate Tower

Site of Gateway

← TO ALWINTON

Steep Slope

TO ROTHBURY →

before her once or twice a day to look at. She has within the castle 22 gocons of cloth of gold and silks, and yet she has sent to Edinburgh for more, which have come today. She is going in all haste to have a gown of purple velvet, lined with cloth of gold, gown of bright crimson velvet, furred with ermine, three gowns more and three kirtles of satin. These five or six days she has no other mind than to look at her apparel".

In 1585 the castle was in a bad state of repair and the remains became a quarry from which the village of Harbottle was built.

Like most Norman castles Harbottle had a donjon or keep, a barbican or gate tower, an inner and an outer bailey, enclosed by curtain walls. Around the keep was a ditch and around the whole enceinte was another ditch crossed by a draw-bridge. The engraving here illustrated shows the north-west face of the keep with its arrow holes as it appeared in 1903.

When the old castle fell into ruin some of the stone was used to build the new Harbottle Castle, a fine 17th century house which can be seen when approaching the village from the east. This dignified mansion was built by the Widdringtons but has been considerably enlarged since. We show a view of the house in 1903.

HARNHAM HALL

In 1415 we read that the fortalice of Harnhamhall, which was two miles from Belsay, belonged to Robert Swinburne. It was in a very strong natural position. On the north and west are precipitous sand-

21

stone rocks and on the south a steep glacis. The neck of land on the east was protected by a high wall. The tower remains but the windows were altered in the 16th and 17th centuries. Originally Harnham was part of the barony of Bolam but in 1667 it came into the hands of Major Babington, Governor of Berwick whose wife Katherine was the daughter of Sir Arthur Haselrigg. To this lady the fame of Harnham Hall is chiefly due. Kate Babington was celebrated for her good looks and her portrait was inserted in the "Book of Beauty" of that period. It is said, too, that an order was issued, during her residence in Sunderland, that when she entered a cook's shop she should not eat sixpenny pies in public, but in a private room, that she "be not stared at of the people". She was a strong Puritan and she incited the blacksmith's son to pull the Vicar out of his pulpit. On the Restoration he excommunicated both of them. When the young man died he had to be buried in the garden. Katherine was refused burial in the churchyard and had to be interred in a vault in the garden. Her lead coffin was

Harnham Hall ·· The Chimney Look-out ··

stolen by some itinerant muggers but the inscription on the tomb remains. It reads:—

> "Here lyeth the body of Mdam Babington, who was laid in
> this sepulchre on the 9th September 1670
>
> > My time is past, as you may see,
> >
> > I viewed the dead as you do me;
> >
> > Or long you'll be as low as I,
> >
> > And some will look on thee."

Harnham Hall contains many interesting reminders of the Babington family. In one room is their coat of arms with the motto "Foy est tout". On the ceiling of another room their crest is shown in plaster, it is a dragon's head, and the room is named the Dragon Room after it. The Hall has a finely ornamented doorway and on the roof is the famous chimney look-out. There are a number of dates on the building the earliest of 1590 is on the lintel of a farm building.

The village of Harnham is an attractive place and its site the historian Wallis fancied bore some resemblance to "one of the fine towered hills in the pictures of Nicholas Poussin".

HARTINGTON HALL

HARTINGTON TOWER

"At Hartenton hall ys a stronge bastell house of the Inherytaunce of Sir John Fenwyke, in good reparacons", so write the commissioners of 1541. Here it was that Meg of Meldon, the miserly lady of Sir William Fenwick, principally resided and amassed her treasure. (See

Meldon Tower). Half a mile to the north is *Gallows Hill.* "Tradition tells us of two brothers of the name of Reay, men of Cyclopean strength of stature, who farmed Gallows Hill, and in the twilight of a summer's morning, one of them, seeing a band of moss-troopers driving off their cattle, rose, ran after them, and attacked them single-handed; but before his brother could get to his assistance the thieves had mastered him, and "cut him into collops", which his friends collected and carried home in a sheet". *Hodgson.* The remains of the tower are probably incorporated in the present Hall.

HEPPLE TOWER

Hepple was the most important lordship in the parish of Rothbury. The barony was created by King John in favour of Ivo de Vesci but later it came into the joint possession of the De Hepples and De Talbois. In 1372 Walter de Talbois, had to prove at an Inquisition in Newcastle that he was of full age. The following curious evidence was given. "Robert de Louthre deposed that the said Walter was 21 years old on the Feast of the Purification last past; that he was born at Hephal and baptised in the church at Routhbury. He recollected the day because he was a god-father. John de Walington recollected the day because he had a son baptized there on the same day. John Lawson recollected the day because he had a son buried there the same day."

Hepple Tower is first mentioned in 1415 as the tower of Sir Robert Ogle. An article published in 1853 tells us:— "Hepple Castle at present is in the last stage of dilapidation. About half a century ago the exterior walls of a strong and stately tower were still standing tolerably entire, which had probably been the manor-house of the proprietors of Hepple, as it is said the court leet of Hepple lordship was held here in former times, until the castle, being ruined by the

HEPPLE.

Scots, was totally abandoned by the lord, who removed his court to Great Tosson, where the tenants of Hepple and the demesne annually convene to this day. In erecting a few farmsteads an effort was made to demolish the remaining fragments of this strong tower, but the attempt, after repeated trials, was relinquished by the workmen, who found it easier to cut stones from the hardest quarry then to separate them from the cement."

The remnants of the tower surviving to-day were once part of a longer building. The vaulted basement measures internally 26 x 17 feet, with walls six feet thick. It is 17 feet high with provisions for a loft which was supported on stone corbels. The entrance is a pointed door on the south with a meutriere (murder hole) above. There appear to have been two upper storeys. There were once several bastles in Hepple. Mackenzie says that about 1750 the village consisted of several strong old houses.

HEPSCOTT

Hepscott Hall stands north of the Hepscott burn which a little lower down is called Sleekburn. It is recorded that a hall was built here before 1603 around an old tower.

HIRST PELES

Warburton's survey of 1715 mentions two ancient peles at North Hirst (near Ashington). The "castle" of Hirst was still there in Hodgson's day incorporated into a farmhouse. Nothing is really known of these two towers.

HOPE PEEL

The remains of this pele are shown on the Ordnance Survey map (4.E.7) as two miles east of Cragside (Rothbury).

KIRKHARLE TOWER

The village of Kirkharle is five miles N.W. of Capheaton. The tower here is first mentioned in 1722. Kirkharle was a manor included in the barony of Bolbeck and was held in 1365 by Sir Robert de Harle and later by the Loraines. The tower was demolished at the end of the 19th century with the exception of the east end which was converted into a farmhouse.

KIRKLEY TOWER

The name is derived from Celtic "cryc" signifying hill and English "law" meaning the same. The duplication arose when the earlier meaning was forgotten. Of the tower mentioned in the list of 1415 not even the site is known. Kirkley Hall, now an agricultural college, is pleasantly situated on the southern bank of the Blyth surrounded by a landscaped park. The hall was originally built in 1632 by Cuthbert Ogle whose arms are carved above the modern doorway. The house was largely rebuilt after a fire in 1928. West of the hall on a grassy mound is a simple stone obelisk. It commemorates the "Great and Glorious Revolution of 1688".

KIRKWHELPINGTON TOWER

The vicar's tower here is first mentioned in 1541. It was small, measuring 27 by 15 feet, with walls 5 feet thick. One of the walls was incorporated in the old vicarage and in Hodgson's time stood 20 feet high.

LINBRIG PELE

Linbrig was the most western pele in Upper Coquetdale. It is first mentioned by Leland in 1538. He writes — "Coquet cummithe by herbatell a goodly castle and thens to linne briggs sumtyme of stone now fallen. Therabout was great buyldinge but now desolation". Three years later the border commissioners reported:—

At the Lynne Brigge there hathe bene a stone house of thin-herytaunce of one Rogr Horseley but yt was bronnte and casten downe by the Scottes in tyme paste, and the owner hathe gathered the stones thereof unto a place of more strength nere unto the same, and to buylde a newe bastell house as his power wyll serve him Intendeth.

Of Roger Horsley's stone house there is now no trace but Dippie Dixon says that in his time (1903) there was in a field east of Linbridge called Ducket Knowe a mound of stones, but since Ducket means Dovecote it is probable the lord's dovecote was here and not Horsley's pele tower.

LITTLE HARLE TOWER

The remains of this tower are incorporated in a large Victorian mansion. It has been elaborately modernised. In the survey of 1541 it is described as "in good reparations". It formerly belonged to the De Harles, passing successively into the hands of the Fenwicks and the Aynsleys. In the mansion is an interesting fireplace which came from Anderson House, Newcastle.

LITTLE SWINBURN TOWER

This tower is now a ruin which still shows the doorway and part of the spiral staircase. Not mentioned in 1415 but in 1541 it is said that "at lytle Swyneburne is a little towre of the inheritance of Thomas Mydleton of Belso, esqui' decayed in the roofes." Our illustration shows the tower as it was 150 years ago.

From a drawing by   the late Mr Edward Swinburne.

LOW FAIRNLEY BASTLE

This house now used as a farm building is near the meeting of the Fairnley and Ottercops burns (Rothley). The date on the head of the doorway, 1713, is probably when alterations were made. There is no vault but the hearth was carried on corbelling.

Low Fairnley Pele.

Pele Tower Long Horsley

LONGHORSLEY TOWER

The massive old pele tower at Longhorsley is a striking landmark on the road from Morpeth to Rothbury. When, and by whom, this tower was erected we do not know. It is not mentioned in the list of Border towers in 1415. Robert Horsley, who died in 1445, occupied the tower of Thernham, now called Farnham, in Coquetdale. It was probably built in the 16th century. At the turn of the century it was used as a Catholic manse but is now a private residence. The pele is a massive tower measuring 42 by 30 feet, of four storeys. The vaulted basement measures 22 ft. x 8 ft., and the original door on the south side has been turned into a window. At the east end are two smaller vaults, one of which leads into a seventeenth century wing. The ground

Arms of the Lords of Meldon.

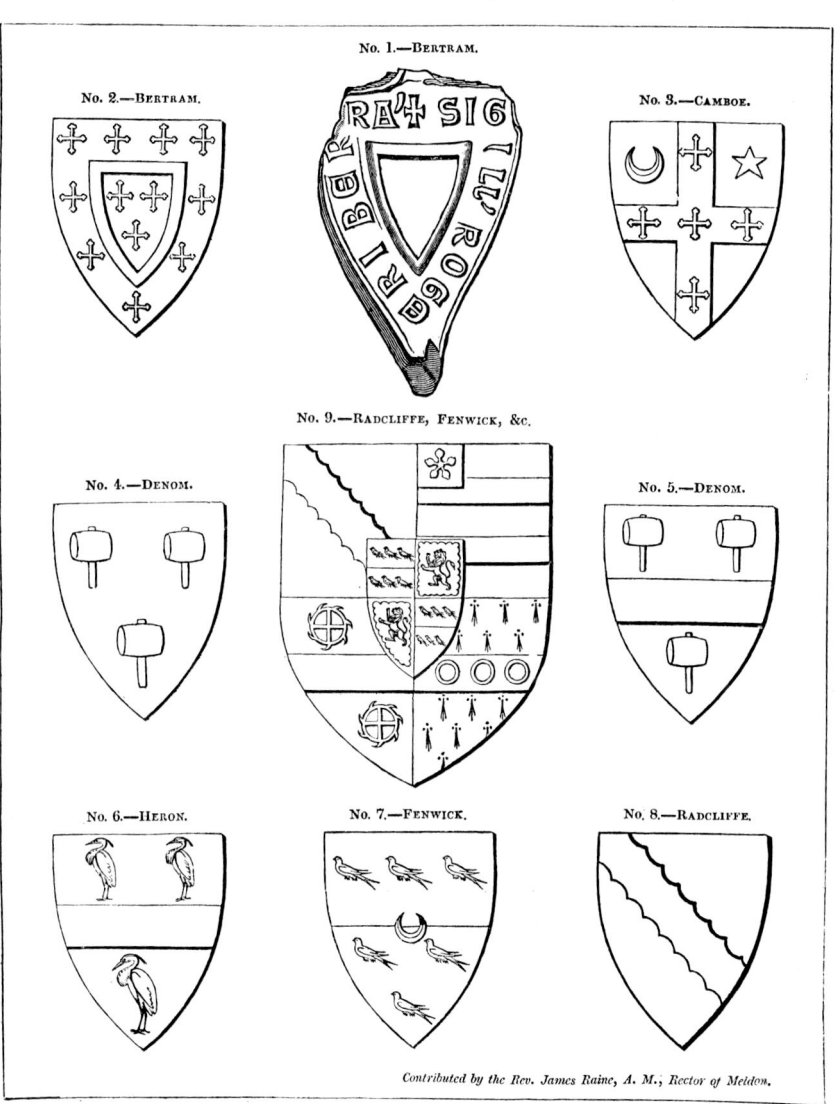

No. 1.—BERTRAM.

No. 2.—BERTRAM.

No. 3.—CAMBOE.

No. 9.—RADCLIFFE, FENWICK, &c.

No. 4.—DENOM.

No. 5.—DENOM.

No. 6.—HERON.

No. 7.—FENWICK.

No. 8.—RADCLIFFE.

Contributed by the Rev. James Raine, A. M., Rector of Meldon.

floor of this addition is known as "The Lady's Room". The three upper floors are of little interest apart from a fine fireplace with a large stone lintel which was discovered fifty years ago when the wainscoting was removed. A newel staircase leads from the basement to the battlements which are in a perfect state of preservation. They are rather low and designed partly for ornamentation. All the windows are renewals but appeared to have had hood-moulds originally.

LOW TREWITT TOWER (Rothbury)

The tower here, belonging to Hugo Calon, is first mentioned in 1415. Now no trace remains. North of Trewitt Farm are mounds in a field probably the site of the tower and nearby are similar mounds supposed to be of the village. In the west gable of the farmhouse is a small 14th century window which was discovered and built in to preserve it. This is most likely the only remnant of the old tower.

MELDON TOWER

We first read of Meldon Tower in 1415 when it belonged to Nicholas Heron. Hodgson says fragments of the tower could be seen in his day 150 yards south east of the church. Today nothing remains. It is associated with the famous Meg o' Meldon. Meg, or rather Margaret Selby, was the daughter of Alderman William Selby, who was sheriff of Newcastle in 1564. She married Sir William Fenwick of Wallington, whose effigy can still be seen in Meldon church. Legend says that Meg was a hard fisted miser. As part of her dowry she had a mortgage on Meldon Tower. She foreclosed on the penniless squire and the last of the Herons to live at Meldon departed a broken man. Meg's ghost can still be seen at Meldon bridge (of which only a fragment survives). Before dying she buried her treasure in a well near the tower and it still remains to be discovered.

MITFORD CASTLE

It is probable that the castle of Mitford existed in 1138. Richard of Hexham describing the advance of David of Scotland refers to Mitford as the "oppidum" of William Bertram. "Oppidum" usually means a fortified town but here obviously refers to the castle which was the head of the barony of Mitford. In 1215 it was seized by the Flemish troops of King John who laid waste the north "burning without mercy all their towns and oppressing the inhabitants with tortures to extort money", but they appear to have left Mitford intact. In 1315 it was held by Sir Gilbert de Middleton and a group of bandits who made the castle their headquarters, pillaging the countryside, and seizing prisoners whom they held to ransom. The castle was taken by a ruse by a band of men under the leadership of Sir William Felton and Sir Thomas Heton. But a few years later the castle seems to have been dismantled. It is described in 1327 as the "site of a castle wholly burned" which had been held in chief by the service of a baron and

Drawn & Lithographed by R. Mackreath.

Printed by C.Hullmandel.

REMAINS OF THE ANCIENT CASTLE OF MITFORD

31

31s. 4d. cornage to the king's castle of Newcastle upon Tyne. Its stones were later used to build the Jacobean mansion house whose ruins still stand, and the early 19th century Hall.

The castle stands on the south bank of the Wansbeck on a natural sandstone hill, At the beginning of the 12th century there was almost certainly a wooden motte and bailey castle here. Within a few years a massive stone wall was built around the top of the motte forming a shell keep curved on the south with the other three sides straight. About the beginning of the 13th century a stone keep of five sides was built inside the inner ward, or shell keep. Although small it almost filled the inner ward. This is the only five-sided keep in England. The vaulted basement, consisting of two chambers, is all that remains. The curtain wall of the outer ward was probably built a little before the keep. The towers, gatehouse and postern have all gone as well as the buildings which would be found in the courtyard. The site of the cruciform chapel has been discovered. Beyond the north wall was a barmkin but all traces of its wall have disappeared if it ever was defended. The main entrance was at the South end of the outer bailey.

MORPETH CASTLES AND TOWERS

There have been a number of fortresses at Morpeth none of which has played an important part in Northumbrian history.

CASTLE ON HA' HILL

The first castle here was built on Ha' Hill. It was a motte and bailey type. The motte was on the hill the bailey lay to the west. It is probably first mentioned in 1905 as a small stronghold and in 1138 is referred to in connection with the foundation of the Abbey of Newminster. Ranulph de Merley entertained here the eight monks from Fountains Abbey whom he had invited north to found a new monastery.

The chronicle-poem of Geffrei Gaimar, written about 1140 tells, us how it was captured by Rufus in 1095, during his campaign against Robert of Mowbray, the Earle of Northumberland.

> Then he (Rufus) took Morpeth a strong castle,
> Which stood on a hill,
> Above Wansbeck it stood,
> William of Morlei held it.

The timber castle was probably replaced by a stone tower in the middle of the 12th century. However in 1251 the castle was destroyed by King John; as Leland says, he " bet downe Morpeth Castle whiche standeth by Morpeth Towne". It was not rebuilt. In the 13th century another castle was built on the hill to the south. Whether it was built by the Merlays who held the land until 1271 or by the Greystocks, we do not know.

Of this castle only the Gate-house and part of the curtain wall remains. It is mentioned in 1310, 1343 and in the List of 1415, as belonging to "Baron de Graystock". The castle had passed by marriage from the Merlays to the Greystokes. It was one of the Greystokes, William known as the Good Baron, who built the Gate-House. The gate tower has a four centred arch with a pointed tunnel-vault. There are machicolations above the outer entrance. The parapet is corbelled and has embattled angle turrets. The pitched roof and windows are modern. The fragmentary curtain walls are much older than the 15th century tower and enclose a bailey measuring 82 x 53 yards.

In 1644 it was described as being "a ruinous hole, not tenable by nature, far less by art". Yet so strong was it that even than a party of 500 Scots who had been left to garrison it by the Parliamentary army were able to stand a siege of twenty days against an army of 2,700 men led by the Marquis of Montrose. The governor banked up the outer gate with earth to prevent it being blown in by a mine and successfully repulsed all attacks. The trenches thrown up by the attacking forces may still be seen to the west of the castle. Montrose placed his guns on the Ha' Hall. A number of the canon balls which were fired at the time were discovered by workmen in 1836.

The castle came by marriage to the famous "Belted Will" Howard of Naworth Castle whose descendant the Earl of Carlisle still owns the barony.

There was also a tower at Morpeth which stood on the site of the old prison, that is behind the huge gatehouse of the police station. Nothing remains of it today.

33

Ruins of Fingwith

Remains of Maybole Castle

Eng. by Mitchell

Arms on Sergeants Mace.

34

Clock Tower, Morpeth.

The Town Belfry is in Oldgate. It was built in the 15th century but has been added to. It was a signal tower but could also be used as a refuge.

NETHERWITTON TOWER

The village of Netherwitton, lying among woods and rich pastures, is 7 miles north west of Morpeth. The tower here is first mentioned in 1415. A tablet in the north wall of Netherwitton Hall, bearing the arms of Thornton and the inscription "anno Regis Edwardi Quinti" (in the year of King Edward V) probably belonged to this earlier building, and refers to some repairs or additions which were made to it in 1483. Roger Thornton, the famous 14th century merchant of Newcastle was born in the neighbouring hamlet of Thornton and his family owned Netherwitton for many generations.

Netherwitton Hall was built about 1700 the architect being Robert Trollop, who also built Capheaton and the Old Exchange at Newcastle. At the rear of the house some old stonework is probably part of the medieval tower.

Half a mile north of Netherwitton on the Devil's Causeway are the foundations of what is claimed to be a tower. However nothing is known of the scanty remains and what the original building was is doubtful.

NEWTOWN BASTLE (Rothbury)

Newtown, now only a farmstead, stands on the south side of the Coquet at the foot of the Simonside hills. Dixon tells us that the ruined walls of the only remaining bastle house of the hamlet stood, in his day, on a knoll overlooking a small stream.

NORTH MIDDLETON TOWER

Although this tower, in Hartburn parish is mentioned in the list of 1415 as belonging to Robti Ogille Chir, nothing else is known about it.

NUNYKIRK TOWER

Two miles north west of Netherwitton is Nunnykirk Hall a building of great elegance and a classical masterpiece, built by John Dobson in 1825. It stands on the site of an old pele tower. Nunykirk was granted by Ranulph de Merlay to Newminster Abbey. Before the Dissolution of the monasteries a tower was erected to defend the grange here. In 1547 it was in the possession of Sir Thomas Gray. Nothing now remains.

Ogle Castle

OGLE CASTLE

All that remains of Ogle Castle is incorporated with a 16th century manor house, which is situated seven miles south west of Morpeth. A plate inserted in the west wall tells us:— "Ogle Castle, for the building whereof a patent was granted anno 15th Edward III, Anno Domini

1341 which, together with the barony of Ogle, now belongs to the Ogles of Kirkley, who are descended from the third Baron Ogle". In 1783 it is thus described:— "Part of a circular tower adjoins to the east of the present farmhouse, which stands on the site of the castle: the windows of this tower are very small, topped with pointed arches, the whole remains carrying a countenance of very remote antiquity. The ground wherein the chief part of the castle has stood is square, guarded by a double moat, divided by a breat-work of mason-work. The walls are quite levelled with the ground, and the moat almost grown up." There is evidence of an original L-plan because there are the remains of a spiral staircase which is outside the square tower. The house contains several original fireplaces.

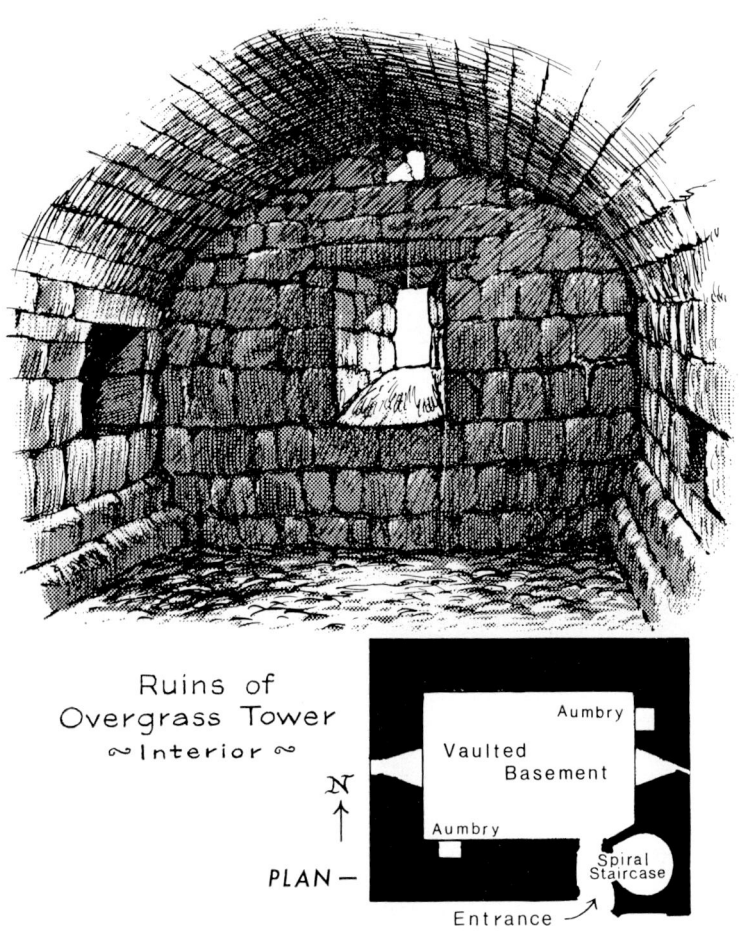

Ruins of
Overgrass Tower
∾ Interior ∾

N
↑

PLAN —

Aumbry

Vaulted
Basement

Aumbry

Spiral
Staircase

Entrance ⟶

OVERGRASS TOWER

South east of Newmoor Hall (Longframlington) the ruins are overgrown with vegetation. It is a small, oblong tower not mentioned in the 1415 list and nothing is known of its history. It was probably built in the 15th century. Part of the vaulting and barmkin remain. Internally the vault measures 23 ft. 6 ins. x 16 ins. and the walls are six feet thick.

Fireplace in Errington Pele Tower, Ponteland.

PONTELAND CASTLE

The Blackbird Inn is formed from a 17th century manor house and a 14th century pele tower. The tall projecting gable in the centre, with its mullioned windows, is the Jacobean house built by Mark Errington, whose initials appear above the doorway. Adjoining on the south is the ancient Ponteland Castle which was altered by Mark Errington to make it more comfortable at the time when he was building his manor house. This tower has been expertly restored to form part of the Blackbird Inn. The basement of the tower is vaulted and a newel staircase leads to the first floor. The basement has been altered by the addition of a fireplace, mullioned window, and a new entrance, and the stonework has been plastered over. The first floor is a fine spacious room with a large decorated fireplace in the centre of which is carved a cross and the initials M.E. When this fireplace was remodelled in the

17th century the huge chimney stack which dominates the exterior was probably built. The second floor no longer exists. A wall-opening high in the gable, a loop in the south west corner now filled with leaded panes, and a meutriere in the thickness of the wall still survives to remind us of less peaceful days. The old tower, the Jacobean house, and the modern building on the north all blend harmoniously to form one of our finest inns, a credit to those who restored it.

The Blackbird Inn, Ponteland.

PONTELAND TOWER

The history of the vicar's pele, which stands in the rectory garden, is unknown. It is a three-storeyed ruin heavily repaired in the 18th century.

ROTHBURY CASTLE

For more than a century after the Conquest Rothbury was in the possession of the Crown. It wasn't until 1204 that King John handed it over to the lords of Warkworth. On the attainder of the Earl of Northumberland in 1461 the lordship of Rothbury was granted for life to Sir Robert Ogle, warden of the East Marches. Although we have no record it is almost certain that the earl of Northumberland would erect a fortress in the important manor of Rothbury. Camden described it as a "brave castle" which tradition says stood on the Haa Hill (Hall Hill) the name of which is preserved in Haw Hill House. A

39

sketch published by D. Dippie Dixon shows Rothbury Hall, the church, and bridge, with the old lock-up on the left as they appeared in 1843. The view shows that the castle consisted of a square tower with east and west gables. The prison which is often mentioned in medieval times (*e.g.* in 1256) probably refers to the dungeon like chambers which formed the basement of the old building. In 1661 "Rothbury Hall" was occupied by "William Thirlwall, gentleman". As late as the 1850's the upper portions were still inhabited but in 1869 the ruins were cleared away to provide an extension to the churchyard. Not a trace now remains.

ROTHLEY CASTLE

The two towers of Rothley Castle were built in 1776 as an eye-catcher. Originally gigantic statues stood at the corners. The towers crown the summit of the crags, 843 feet above sea level, and command an extensive view of the surrounding country. They were erected by Sir Walter Blackett of Wallington.

ROTHLEY TOWER

The tower is in the list of 1541 and was built by John Buttler, abbot of Newminster in 1541. Nothing now remains.

RYAL TOWER

This tower is only referred to once when in 1519 it was given to John Fenwick by his father. Its site is unknown.

SHARPERTON PELE

Sharperton is a hamlet on the left bank of the Coquet, the road from Rothbury to Harbottle passing through the township. Here a ruined stone building is all that remains of the early bastle. Enough of the lower storey stands to show that it was not vaulted.

SHORT FLATT TOWER

Near the junction of the road from Bolam with that from Middleton is Shortflatt Tower, a picturesque old building on the south bank of a stream called the Howburn. It was originally a pele-tower, crenellated in 1305, and called a fortalice in 1415. It was the property of the Raymes family and later the Fenwicks. A house was later attached to the tower, with a big stepped chimney breast and a 17th century doorway. The lower story of the tower remains unaltered with its characteristic tunnel vault. There are also battlements with rainspouts below them.

STANTON TOWER

Stanton Old Hall, two miles south of Longhorsley, is now partly in ruins. It has had a chequered history. Hodgson says that it was used as a shop, a workhouse and granaries, and one "man lives and makes a living out of the walled garden". In 1677 William Veitch the Covenanter lived here. He was persecuted under the Stuarts. Here is an account of an attempt to arrest him.

"Upon the second Sabbath of August, 1677, one of the justices with his party came to the foregates, but Mr. Ogle (of Causey Park)

The West Front

41

Stanton Tower

with his party came to the postern gate and broke up a nailed door about three of the clock in the afternoon without even demanding an entrance and bursting up another door which the minister's wife was shutting until her husband escaped. In the meantime, the minister got into a hole within the lining of a great window, which had been made on purpose for the whole room was lined about with wainscot".

The oldest portion of Stanton Hall is a pele which is oblong with a south projection. Its date is unknown. The rest of the building is Tudor or early 17th century work, with hood-moulded mullioned windows. The west front has two bays with curly open pediments of the 18th century.

THROPTON TOWER

Thropton Tower is first mentioned in 1415 as belonging to William Grene. In 1509 it was held by Sir Edward Radcliffe and contained a garrison of 16 men for defence against the Scots. It may have been part of Thropton Old Hall which was demolished in 1811 to make room for the Catholic Presbytery. But there still remains at the west end of the village a well preserved pele tower with walls five feet thick. It has been modernised and is still occupied. It is of two stories with a vaulted basement and an original window in the west gable shows there was always an attic. There are two original first floor windows.

South Front.
WALLINGTON HALL
G. Hall

WALLINGTON TOWER

Of the medieval castle of Wallington only the foundations can be seen in the present cellars and the paving stones in the small north courtyard may have belonged to the original building. It was the property of John Grey in 1326 but later passed to the de Strothers. Alan de Strother is recorded as its owner in 1352. In the list of 1415 it belonged to William Strother. In the reign of Henry IV Sir John Fenwick married a Strother heiress and thus acquired the estate. In

WALLINGTON in NORTHUMBERLAND,
the Seat of Sir Walter Blackett Bar.t

44

the middle of the 16th century the Fenwicks, like the owners of Chipchase and Belsay, added a Tudor house to their medieval fortress. The Border Survey, of 1541 described Wallington as a stronge toure and a stone house in good reparacions". In 1684 Sir John Fenwick sold the estate to Sir William Blackett a Whig businessman of Newcastle with interests in coal, lead mining and shipping. The Fenwicks were Jacobites and the last owner of Wallington was executed in 1697 for plotting the assassination of William III. Sir William demolished the medieval castle and Tudor mansion house and built the courtyard house whose exterior we see today, almost unchanged. However his grandson, Sir William Calverley Blackett, from 1727 onwards entirely remodelled the interior.

WARTON BASTLES

David Dippie Dixon tells us that during the troublous days on the borders the chief inhabitants at Warten in Upper Coquetdale lived in bastle houses which are not mentioned in the list of border towers. A diarist of 1717 refers to the "several old towers thereabouts for defence against the incursions of ye Scotts".

WEST THORNTON TOWER (Hartburn Parish)

The farm of West Thornton is probably built on the site of this tower. Formerly there were a chapel and manor house here surrounded by a barmkin. But in 1715 the tower was gone. A survey of that year describes only a "ruinous chapell and a callebet well" as being here.

WEST WHELPINGTON PELE

The village is now a heap of ruins. It once consisted of two rows of houses enclosing a large green in the centre of which stood a strongly-built pele, about 23 by 21 feet inside. Nearby was a small circle probably the site of a cock-pit. The pele is mentioned in the parish registers up to 1715.

WHALTON PELE

Writing in 1897 W. Tomlinson remarks that "the old bastle-houses, of which the village was formerly composed, have all disappeared since the Border reivers ceased to trouble the land". There are slight remains of an old pele incorporated in the present rectory.

WITTON SHIELD TOWER

A mile and a half east of Netherwitton in the farmstead of Witton Shield stand the remains of a late tower, if indeed it can be so called since it is probably only a manor house. It is three storeys high and has a south projection which contains a doorway and spiral stair. A similar doorway leads from it into the house and is dated 1608 with the letters N.T. which are supposed to be the initials of Sir Nicholas Thornton. In one of the upper rooms was once a Roman Catholic chapel.

WHITTON TOWER

For many centuries it was the residence of the rectors of Rothbury. Before the first world war it was turned into a Children's Hospital which it remains today. The house now consists of the old pele with various later additions on two sides. The pele tower was built in the 14th century but the upper part was probably added by Alexander Cook who did a good deal of restoration when he was rector of Rothbury in the 15th century.

The tower is unique in having vaulted rooms on the first and second floors. The reason is that due to the slope of the ground its height changes from 42 feet on the south side to 60 feet on the north. This allowed entrance on two floors. The ground floor room has walls more than nine feet thick and the entrance has the unusual feature of two doors at either end of the passage. The well here is three feet in diameter and fifteen feet deep. Entrance to the floor above is by a square hatchway in the roof. In this first floor sitting room a large mullioned window of three lights has replaced a small opening in the south wall. A restored shoulder headed door in the corner opens on to an old newel-stair up to the second floor. This newel stair has many mason's marks and extends to the top of the tower. During alterations in 1894 a recess was revealed which may have been a secret room as well as a piscina carved with oak leaves.

The tower was altered and repaired at various times and extensive additions made in the eighteenth and nineteenth centuries.

Doorway, Woodhouses Bastle.

WOODHOUSES BASTLE

It is sometimes claimed, without any proof, that it is the unfinished "stronge pele" which Roger Hangingshaws began to build 'at a place called the hare clewgh" before 1541. The date on the lintel of 1602 with the initials WP. BP and TAM give us the time of its building, making it the last erection of its kind in Coquetdale. Its plan is the usual Tudor strong house, 30 ft x 17 ft in size with a vaulted ground floor. In the 18th century a one storeyed cottage was added. Both were in ruins when J. T. Dixon made the following sketch in 1886 but they were restored in 1904.

PICTURE PIONEERS by *G. Mellor*. The history of the Movies in Northern England. Illustrated. **£1·50**

BANNER PARADE. The old banners of the Durham miners. Size eleven by nine inches. Twenty-four pages. **60p**

HISTORY OF BERWICK UPON TWEED by *John Fuller*, 1799. Facsimile. 688 pages. **£3·50**

BIRDS OF THE FARNES. A magnificent book with twelve drawings in full colour by *R. Embleton*. Text by *Peter Hawkey*. **60p**

BEWICK GLEANINGS by *Julia Boyd*. 1886. Facsimile limited to 800 copes, 288 pages. **£3·50**
This miscellany is by the daughter of a Novocastrian who as a boy had known Bewick. It contains impressions from numerous Bewick woodblocks as well as some of his work on copper plates.

A HISTORY OF COAL, COKE AND COALFIELDS AND THE MANUFACTURE OF IRON IN THE NORTH OF ENGLAND by *W. Fordyce*. 1860. Reprint. Folio size. 260 pages. 34 illustrations. (includes Hair's *Views of Northern Collieries*). **£7·00**

HISTORY OF NORTHUMBERLAND by *John Hodgson*. Vol. 2. Elsdon, Wallington, Hartburn, Whalton, Redesdale. 434 pages. 24 illustrations. **£7·00**

SONGS OF NORTHUMBRIA edited by Denis Weatherley. Size eleven inches by eight and a half inches. All songs with music for piano and guitar. **70p**

A TREE WITH ROSY APPLES by *Sid Chaplin*. Illustrated by Norman Cornish. 160 pages. A second collection of Sid Chaplin's north country essays and stories. It follows his successful *Smell of Sunday Dinner*. **£2·10**

NATURAL HISTORY IN NORTHUMBERLAND AND DURHAM With 272 pages and 117 illustrations, Henry Tegner presents the most comprehensive account to date of every aspect of Northumbrian natural history. **£3·50**
